RUDE RAGE

Incivility in Verse

JOEL FARSON

**Illustrations
by
Jeremy Farson**

Copyright © 2015, 2011 Joel Farson

Cover design and illustrations by Jeremy Farson

Second edition

ISBN-13: 9781497418134
ISBN: 1497418135

Kindle Edition ebook
and
Audible Audiobook
also at
Amazon.com

RUDE RAGE

CONTENTS

It Doesn't Have to Be This Way 1
Aspiring Down 8
Barbie's Revenge 17
Chuck 25
Gold Digger 30
Fan Male 36
Cul-de-Sac Crusader 39
The Too-Muchness of Everything 43
Corporate Cheaters 48
Urban Sprawl 54

This book is best read *out loud*.

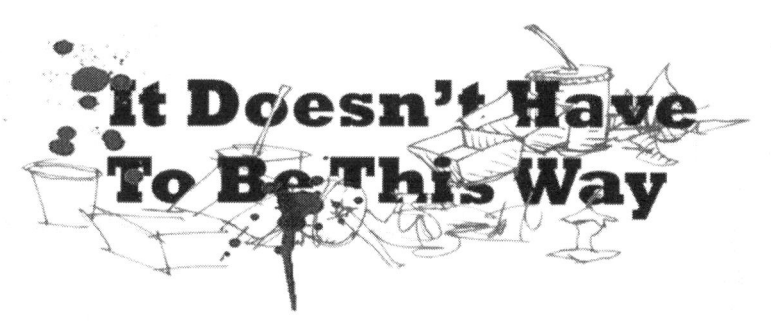

It Doesn't Have To Be This Way

Things are crazy in the world today,
But it doesn't have to be this way.
There was a time in small-town America
When every Tom, Dick, Harry, and Erica
Said "Hello" to each other when they passed on the street,
Made eye-contact, and were happy to meet.
Folks walked to the post office and to the store,
And sugar was borrowed from neighbors next door.
Neighborhood ladies gossiped for hours,
And kindly old men sang in the shower.
Homes were modest, yards were spacious,
Streets were safe, and people were gracious.
Porches were peopled and doors were unlocked;
Kids *walked* to school and no one was shocked.
An old man could tousle a little boy's hair
Without incurring a paranoid stare.

There was no stigma to riding the bus,
And children did chores without too much fuss.

Children built forts inside leafy bowers,
With rocks for walls and trees for towers.
Kids climbed trees, played ball in the park,
Running around until it got dark—
Baseball, football, a game of tag,
Hide-and-Go-Seek, and Capture-the-Flag.
When it got dark they ran home for dinner.
(That's one reason back then they were thinner.)
Children with suntans and scrapes on their knees
Came home hungry and ate all their peas.
Families at dinner sat 'round the table
And talked to each other. (They didn't watch cable.)
Parents taught children to be polite
And know the difference between wrong and right.
Etiquette, manners, and decorum—
Back then people didn't ignore 'em.

Out on the porch on warm summer nights,
Folks told stories by the twilight,
Or got lost in a book, reading for pleasure.
Those are the times they truly would treasure.
Lying in a hammock, nicely reclined,

Reader and author became intertwined.
Books were borrowed from the library,
Just like in *Little House on the Prairie*.

After dinner, to digest their food,
People took walks, improving their mood.
Families would stroll under the stars
Observing Orion, Venus, and Mars.

We don't stroll much these days, after twilight;
We're holed-up indoors by a flickering blue light.
In our neighborhoods nobody walks;
We watch TV and nobody talks.
An increasing sense of alienation
And loneliness grips the nation.
Sometimes we feel so alone
Our neighborhood's like a twilight zone.
When it gets dark, folks withdraw.
(You'd think we lived under martial law.)
Crime in the media is magnified,
So people grow frightened of the world outside.
Once brave pioneers on a wild frontier,
We've now become a culture of fear.
We used to be bold and ready to act.
Now we're afraid to make eye contact.

So, we watch TV in perfect silence,
Un-phased by its bloody violence.
The things we witness with our eyes!
(No wonder something inside us dies.)

Our social skills are almost gone.
We go through life with blinders on.
People don't smile; they don't say "Hi!"
They divert their eyes and walk on by,
As if they're in a kind of trance—
They walk on by without a glance—
Completely closed and unexpressive,
Or are they really passive-aggressive?
"How's it going?" Don't bother asking.
They're on their smart phones multitasking.

And all kids do is text and tweet.
They're awkward with adults they meet.
They can't recall a book they've read.
They want to play video games instead.
Their parents seldom read to them
From Aesop or the Brothers Grimm.
They haven't read Dr. Seuss,
Maurice Sendak, or Mother Goose.
They haven't read Roald Dahl
Or really any books at all.
Their greatest source of erudition

Is by watching television.
In search of instant gratification,
All they do is change the station.
They've got no grit, no country soul.
They argue over the remote control.
On the couch, completely static,
They're the picture of phlegmatic.

Popular culture—violent and sexual—
Has made us anti-intellectual.
We watch TV with its violence perverted.
(If the streets aren't safe it's because they're deserted.)
If you do stroll at night, after a day of hard working,
You won't see your neighbors and you'll feel like you're lurking.
You'll feel the eyes of people staring
As they drive by with headlights glaring.
You'll walk amidst a world of cars
And feel as though you are from Mars.
Sidewalks are lonely and void of life.
(Anyone on them could have a knife!)
We keep our guns loaded, security tightened
In gated communities, but why are we frightened?
In the suburbs, when it's too dark to see,
We think there's a psycho behind every tree.

Yes, crime is real—a societal curse—
But fearing society will just make it worse.
Where's the community and social grace?
Must we jog with cans of mace?
Equip our homes with cameras and lasers?
Conceal and carry guns and tasers?

Vibrant communities once made up the nation.
There were more picnics and less isolation.
We've got to revive our local community
Because crime is deterred by this kind of unity.
Sidewalks are safer when folks are out walking,
Waving to neighbors, stopping and talking.
Such interaction is mentally healthy,
As much for the poor as for the wealthy.

So, after dinner take a walk,
Even just around the block.
Teach your kids violin—
Skills that require discipline.
Give them a little space to be free
To run with their friends and climb a tree.
Do things that make you feel alive.
Ride a bike; don't always drive.
Take a hike; learn to cook;
Catch a fish with a hook.
Build a fort; climb a tree;

RUDE RAGE

Swing on a rope and yell, "Whoopee!"
Chat with a neighbor; *walk* to the store.
Don't let these be things we don't do anymore.

Somewhere we have gone astray,
But it doesn't have to be this way….

Aspiring Down

Johnny didn't read Hardy or Poe;
He didn't read Steinbeck, Dickens, or Stowe.
If you gave him a book, he'd just take a nap.
He couldn't find New Guinea if you gave him a map.
"Yo, that don't matter! I listen to rap!"
His music was angry and full of rage,
With language unfit for a boy of his age.
He wore his pants low, and sideways his hats,
He had a goatee and a couple of tats.
He walked like a rapper wherever he went,
Moving his hands to say what he meant:

"Bow-wow-wow! Yo-yo-yo!
Guns and pimps and bitches and ho's"

RUDE RAGE

Please…. How original! Oh, what a rebel!
Turn up the base! Turn up the treble!
So unique, so incredibly hip!
This baggy, branded, ghetto trip.
With a pit bull and an air of distrust,
Johnny's got to look "hard." *That* is a must.

From the city street to the college dorm,
Everyone's trying not to conform.
But when they all play this game,
They all begin to look the same.
They fail to grasp the enormity
Of this rebellion's mass conformity.
They think they're sticking it to the man,
But it's all part of a marketing plan—
A clever scheme, it's Machiavellian—
The mass marketing of rebellion.
They don't even vote to change the laws—
So many rebels without a cause.

(Some folks vote, rain or shine,
But most don't want to stand in line.
Our soldiers die to spread democracy,
But we don't vote. What hypocrisy!)

Johnny's never heard of Darfur or Rwanda,
But he knew what he liked—his lowered Honda.

Low-profile tires and rims so fat,
It did zero to sixty in six seconds flat.
He zipped through town like a weasel
To the smell of burning gas and diesel.
Passing cars on the right
And following people close and tight.
He sped down the freeway, through traffic he weaved.
He tailgated people because he was peeved.
"Move yo' fat ass! You all drivin' too slow!
My homeys are waitin' at a sideshow!"
A sideshow—for those of you who are curious—
Is like in the movie *The Fast and the Furious;*
Where bad boys gather in illicit places,
Spin cars in "donuts" and have little races;
Blasting their music into the night,
Drinking and driving and running red lights.
Oh, the drama at these intersections
Could land you a month in county corrections.

"Bow-wow-wow! Yo-yo-yo!
Guns and pimps and bitches and ho's"

Oh, how their parents wish they would grow-up,
Or at least get away before the cops would show-up!
But alas, our industry of incarceration.
We imprison more people than any nation.

RUDE RAGE

There's a paradox, though, in serving time
When prison becomes a school for crime.

He's not from the ghetto, not from the hood—
Where Johnny's from is really quite good.
His mother sells real estate—strictly suburban;
His father's a teacher who likes to drink bourbon.
They raised him right, but Johnny is errant—
The first generation to do worse than its parents.
Though he didn't grow up in a slum,
He liked to pretend that's where he was from.
With his posturing and his slang,
His goal in life was to be in a gang.
He walked like a gangster hangin' hard in the ghetto,
Even when walking through a beautiful meadow.
His mother would lecture, but Johnny would frown—
A middle-class kid aspiring down.

With shirt un-tucked and pants at his thighs,
He stood there smirking and rolling his eyes.
His dad is angry, his mom distraught,
Over his drinking and smoking of pot.
Johnny responded, *"Okay, but…"*
Or sometimes simply yelled, *"So what?"*
Entitlement culture is what he is fostering
With his attitude and his posturing.

Near Johnny's house are forests and hills
Where he could escape from society's ills.
Take the dog for a walk, its tail wagging.
He could learn about nature; instead he was
    tagging,
Marking his turf on city blocks
Instead of exploring rivers and rocks.
He felt no attraction or devotion
To the mountains or the ocean.
Finding no solace in silent woods,
He blares music through noisy hoods,
Covers walls with graffiti
And discards litter. He makes the town seedy.
Folks who enjoyed walking through town
Feel like Michael Douglas in *Falling Down*.
Instead of hiking through evergreen glades,
Johnny roams malls and video arcades.
He doesn't like beaches, tide pools, or grottos.
He blows people's heads off playing *Grand Theft Auto*.
Pulling triggers with fingers and thumb,
He kills zombies until he is numb.
"I like video games. They're really fun!
Especially the ones where you shoot guns!"

For all his posturing and acting tough,
He had the body of a cream-puff.

RUDE RAGE

A little bit pudgy, a little bit pasty,
He ate at McDonald's because it was tasty.
A burger and fries is what he bought,
And when he was done threw his trash in the lot.
Even though trashcans abound,
Paper bags were blowing around.
Trashcans were there, but Johnny was lazy:
"Take my trash over there? You gotta be crazy!"
He won't walk to the can—says it's too far—
So he throws his garbage out of his car.
(It's surely an insult to your fellow man
When you don't use the garbage can.)
He thought his actions so benign,
But Johnny really should pay a fine.
It tends to make us feel bitter
When the streets are full of litter.
There is litter everywhere
Because many people just don't care.
Don't these people understand
That America is not a wasteland?

Whatever happened to kids with ambition?
Who did well in school and had good nutrition?
Who woke-up early and delivered the news?
Who tucked-in their shirts and polished their shoes?

It's not that Johnny can't read;
It's something he could do.
He could finish books with speed;
He just doesn't want to.
School is seen as a grind,
Like feeding from a trough.
The kind of work Johnny's assigned
Has turned Johnny off.

When it comes to history,
The sequence is a mystery.
After twelve years he takes a quiz,
Yet still doesn't know what an adverb is.
By the time he finishes high school,
He's turned off to knowledge.
He's had about enough to school,
Now it's time for college.

"Bow-wow-wow! Yo-yo-yo!
Guns and pimps and bitches and ho's"

In the Internet Age curiosity has faded.
Bombarded by media, we are blasé and jaded.
For hours a day we stare at a screen.
It's the Age of Information, and we don't know anything.

One night Johnny was driving while drunk
And almost killed a Jesuit monk.
He fled the scene, but soon was caught.
The police took him in to get his mug-shot.
His parents couldn't post bail,
So they hired a counselor to help this young male.
"Look at me, Johnny, and you'd better listen.
If you don't change, you'll end up in prison!"
The lady asked Johnny why he breaks the rules,
And then asked his parents how he does in school.
"Our Johnny doesn't read, doesn't care for academe;
But we've tried so hard to build his self-esteem."
"Don't criticize him," said the frumpy educator.
"It's the job of the parent to be a motivator.
Encourage his love of music. What instrument
   does he play?"
"He doesn't play an instrument. He raps like
   Dr. Dre."
"Then encourage his poetry. Perhaps he'll
   write a song."
"Well, he didn't write a thing until we took away
   his bong.
He was supposed to write a paper on Chaucer's
   Canterbury Tales.
But what did Johnny write about? Gang culture in
   jails.

His teacher explained this wasn't correct,
So Johnny hit the teacher.... You know—perceived
    disrespect."
"Well if he likes music, perhaps he can dance."
"Oh, he dances all right, when given the chance.
When there's a dance at the high school gym
He sneaks in a bottle of vodka or gin....
Our efforts don't really seem to be working.
He watches girls do a dance called Twerking.
And Johnny dances too, in a manner of speaking,
A depraved little number they like to call
    Freaking!* "

She showed up at the casting call
Dressed up like a Barbie doll.
Others like her, on a mission,
Also waited to audition.
Girls who've dreamt since childhood

Of being stars in Hollywood
Waited in the studio
To dance in a music video.
A contribution to the arts
If only they can get the parts.
Beauty queens and southern belles,
Scantily clad because sex sells.
They're trying hard to convince us
They've moved beyond the Disney Princess.
Generations obsessed with appearance.
(Their college essays lacked coherence.)
Of science and history they are oblivious.
They just want to be lascivious.
And though it sounds a little crass,
The public wants tits and ass.

One girl really is a beauty,
And she can surely shake her booty.
She doesn't ride horses or figure skate,
But she has talents that are innate.
Her sex appeal is in demand.
She is the product; she is the brand.
She made it through the first cut
Because she has a cute butt.
Yet, to insure against rejection,
She gave the director a little affection.
It doesn't take much to seduce her

RUDE RAGE

If you are the artist or producer.
She's not the type to kiss and tell
(But the casting couch is alive and well).

She arrived on set later that week
With instructions to dance like a freak.
A music video for all to see,
And it will play on MTV!
The music has no political leaning,
No social cause or deeper meaning.
It's not Joan Baez or Bob Dylan.
The song is called "We Be Chillin'."
The entire set is a giant party
Of vapid co-eds dancing dirty:
Sexy guys with razor stubble,
Six-pack abs, and heads like a bubble.
All are tan and all are trim;
All are creatures of the gym.
Bouncing to the empty beat,
She joins the other dancing meat
In their wild pelvic thrusts,
Pandering to our animal lusts,
Bumping, grinding, and gyrating—
They look like they are fornicating;
Shaking booty and grabbing crotch.
(We can't condemn it if we like to watch.)

So much, these days, in society
Is an affront to our sense of propriety.
Parents don't want to see their child
On an episode of *Girls Gone Wild*.
"That's me and my friends on spring break,
Flashing our tits out on the lake."
She wears a thong and a C-cup,
(Her parents don't know she's hooking-up.)
She's rebellious, won't relent,
Stay's out late without consent.
Her *Facebook* page is wild-and-woolly.
(Sometimes she's a cyber-bully.)
At the tender age of seventeen,
She is hooked on nicotine.
And with a strange sense of pride,
As if all innocence in her died,
She drives around with a snicker,
Displaying a "Porn Star" bumper sticker.

Gone are the innocent days of the hickey.
Now boys and girls engage in the "quickie."
They "hook-up" with partners who hardly know 'em.
(Do people still write love poems?)
Gone is the mystery in saying "Maybe."
(Her teenage cousin is having babies.)

Romance today is less enjoyed.
Teens are pregnant and unemployed.
Because they hook-up casually,
Now they have an STD.
But as they say in the hood,
"Peace out, Dog. It's all good!"

You know, a librarian who likes to study
Can be very attractive; she needn't be… *unladylike*.
But library books don't pique our lust.
That's why they are collecting dust.
Bouncing bodies titillate,
So we drop the books and take the bait.
With so much sex in the media,
Why read the encyclopedia?

Children see behavior base and low
On the *Jerry Springer Show*—
*"Daddy, why are those people yelling at each
    other?"*
"I'm watching Jerry Springer. Go ask your mother."
*"Mommy, why are those people yelling at each
    other?"*
*"Well, the lady's fighting with her boyfriend, who's
    sleeping with her brother."*
A spectacle of cursing and incivility—

Does our populace have no humility?
Cursin', fightin', lyin' cheatin',
Bigots, perverts, brats, and cretins.
Tales of incest and brutality
Have become our reality.

So, don't rely on Hollywood
To make a wholesome childhood.
Reality shows across the nation
Showcase lying and manipulation.
In a world of decadence and dumbing-down,
No wonder so many kids wear a frown.
No wonder our souls feel forlorn
When bodies are objects in a world of porn.
We're appalled by the obnoxious crowd,
And it's hard to believe, but they're actually proud!
Proud to be part of each new version;
Each one marked by more perversion.
You too can be an actor;
Just eat some bugs on *Fear Factor*.

So, behold our virtuous public forum—
Vulgarity, vice, and indecorum.
Smiling children in Nepal
Are happier than we who watch it all.

RUDE RAGE

Though it seems like exploitation,
Our Barbie doll calls it liberation.
She wears her exhibitionism
As a badge of feminism.
She trades on her great physique
(but hasn't read *The Feminine Mystique*).
"Why on earth burn my bra?
Isn't that against the law?
Does the sex industry enslave us?
Why should I read Angela Davis?"
Call her *Miss* or call her *Ms.*,
She is succeeding in showbiz,
But still earns less than a man.
(She's never heard of Betty Friedan.)
She played with Barbies; she didn't design 'em.
Why should she read Gloria Steinem?

So teenage girls, still just children,
Want to live like Paris Hilton.
Daughters beg their mothers through tears
To let them dress like Brittany Spears.
Raunchy culture spreads like a virus
With each new video by Miley Sirus.

Can't we agree that it's just wrong
For eight-year-olds to wear a thong?

JOEL FARSON

It's no longer incorrect
To model yourself on a sex object.
Yesterday's feminism isn't much fun.
It looks to me like Barbie won.

Chuck

A red-blooded American, his name is Chuck.
His pride and joy is his monster truck.
With Rancho suspension and tires so big,
It takes some climbing to get in his rig.
A chrome tool chest and a rifle rack,
A pinch of Skoal and a cold six-pack,
A bottle of Jack and Marlboro reds;
He likes four-wheeling in dry river beds.
You should see the dust he kicks up
When he floors this awesome pickup!
He hogs up the road and drives like a nut;
He tailgates people and has a big gut.
He is abrasive and when he goes places

JOEL FARSON

He parks in a lot and takes up two spaces.
The truck's not for work; it's all for show.
He likes riding up high, not sitting down low.
He doesn't haul cargo or ply a trade
(But sometimes the truck helps him get laid).

It costs a lot to fill this machine
With so much oil and gasoline.
His macho image requires much gas.
(In some countries he'd be riding an ass.)
Driving alone, he burns up fuel.
(He wouldn't look so macho riding a mule.)
What is, indeed, the true cost of oil
When soldiers die in Mid-East turmoil?

Born in Texas, he likes living large.
His possessions alone could fill up a barge.
"Ya got that right! I like goin' big!"
(Some would say he lives like a pig.)
*"I like livin' large. That's my creed.
I'm from Texas. I ain't no Swede!"*

On weekends he goes off-roading with the boys.
They conquer the mountains on motorized toys,
Climbing up hills with the greatest of ease,
On buggies and bikes and ATV's.

RUDE RAGE

Chuck doesn't care for surfing or skiing.
These sports are too pure—too quiet and clean.

By the end of the day his pistons are pinging,
His saddle is sore and his ears are ringing.
Chuck views nature with utmost impiety,
Partly because it gives him anxiety.
It makes him feel lonely, meager and small.
He must subdue nature to keep walking tall.
He communes with nature by shooting deer.
(If you disapprove, you're probably queer.)
Something about shooting a gun,
Striking fear in a creature and watching it run,
Makes being a sportsman that much more fun!
"Other sports ain't got the same thrill.
It ain't the same when there's nothin' to kill."
He justifies hunting, when he is able,
As a necessary thing to keep meat on the table.
A solemn duty that has to be done
To feed the family (never mind that it's fun).

Speaking of food that he likes to eat,
All of his meals consist of meat.
He gobbles down meat, beer he guzzles;
Chuck has a mullet, his dogs wear muzzles.
"Meat makes a meal." That's his belief,

Having been raised in a culture of beef.
Not too picky, he eats like a goat.
If it is meat, it goes down his throat.
Chuck eats it all; he is a glutton—
Chicken, pork, veal, or mutton.
He eats like a hog; shirts he would stain.
His mouth is a sink; his throat is a drain.
You should've seen Chuck stuffing his gullet.
(Sometimes he gets sauce on his mullet.)
Nothing goes better with domestic beer
Than a char-broiled hunk of Iowa steer.
Don't feed him salad; he's not in the mood.
He don't take kindly to rabbit food.
Don't give him carrots or hearts of romaine.
Cook him some beef over propane.
Give him a burger and a NASCAR race,
But never a bowl of *bouillabaisse*.
And you won't see him sipping a cappuccino
At a café while reading Calvino.
And don't go picnicking at no winery.
He'd rather shoot duck near the oil refinery.

Charred over fire or fried in grease,
All this meat has made him obese.
While people are starving in the Third World,
Chuck ate so much that sometimes he hurled.

RUDE RAGE

Roasted, fried, boiled, or stewed,
Chuck ate so much that sometimes he spewed.
He keeps eating meat even when full.
Chuck doesn't stop; he keeps eating bull.
Chuck, you mustn't eat so much cow!
Good God, man! Stop eating now!

She didn't read Nietzsche, Kafka, or Sartre.
She didn't know much about music or art.
She didn't care to read the great literati.
She read *Cosmo* and was into her body.
She liked watching shows that made her feel bright.
(Her idea of hard news is *Entertainment Tonight*.)
Reading the paper and watching the news
Were not as important as shopping for shoes.
She didn't read Hugo, Bronte, or Mill,
But she knew what she wanted—a big house on the hill.

RUDE RAGE

A "McMansion" in the style of a Tuscan estate
With a circular drive and a big iron gate,
A three-car garage and a beautiful view,
An infinity pool and a big barbeque.
She impressed her friends with the art she displayed.
(Her idea of great painting is Thomas Kincaid.)
She was one of the country club ladies
Driving around in a big black Mercedes.

But she lost this lifestyle. Yes, it is sad.
She now rents a condo and she is mad.
She has to make do and accept it, of course;
For she has just been through an ugly divorce.
A big-shot lawyer who wore a toupee
Fell head-over-heels for this fiancée.
Though some of her parts are surely synthetic,
He thought her beauty was purely genetic.
The rich man was smitten; he was so fond
Of this buxom kitten, this bottle-blonde.
Oft was she pampered, wined and dined.
She was his trophy wife; she was enshrined.

She wasn't in love, though. She married for money.
She put on an act and called him "Honey."
With the passing of time he felt a lingering fear
That there was a chance she wasn't sincere.

JOEL FARSON

He thought his marriage a fairytale
Until he discovered her great betrayal.
She thought fooling him would be a no-brainer,
Till he caught her in bed with her personal trainer!
Moreover, she didn't show any remorse,
So he went to his office and filed for divorce.
She fought him in court, tooth-and-nail,
For equity in the home (pending sale).
She was so mad, and he was so sour,
But being a lawyer, he had the power.
She could no longer buy precious stones,
Expensive furs, and Moet & Chandon.
But she struck one more blow—had sex with the plumber!
And then in the settlement she got the Hummer!
The lawyer was bitter. He couldn't forgive her,
So he drank like a fish and pickled his liver.

Her finances lost, her psyche destroyed,
She is a case for Sigmund Freud.
But driving that Hummer, she feels a great power,
Even in traffic during rush-hour.
In that Hummer she has control,
Like she is cruising out on patrol.
She takes it to work and to the mall
(But never off-road, never at all).
She doesn't haul cargo or drive it in dirt;
She drives to the cleaners to pick up her skirt.

And though the gas tank quickly runs dry,
It's worth the expense—she likes riding high!

Electric cars are nice in principle,
But in that Hummer she is invincible!
It doesn't matter where she is headin'
In that thing she can survive Armageddon!
It makes her feel big and mean.
(Deep down, she thinks it weak to be green.)
Ensconced within her sport utility,
She feels no sense of humility,
And ignores the plight of the lower class
From behind the tinted glass.

On Thursdays she meets the girls for a drink.
They talk about guys over martinis that are pink.
They plug many names into their checklist—
Men with whom they might coexist.
"You'd really like Bill. He is so funny."
"I'm sure he is, but does he have money?"
"If his salary isn't a lot,
What's the point of tying the knot?"
"My husband's a doctor, a really good catch.
I know it's not easy. Have you tried Match*?"*

Some men are good for a romantic tryst,
But after that they are dismissed.
She goes on dates with men who are bright,

JOEL FARSON

Well intentioned, and even polite.
But they don't meet her expectations;
She sees only their limitations.
At the first hint of foul weather,
There is no chance they'll stay together.
She could be happy if not so exclusive,
Then finding love might not be elusive.
But there's little chance she'll ever be a mom
(Or read *The Art of Loving* by Erich Fromm).
For love requires vulnerability,
A giving spirit, and humility.
She protects herself; she puts up a wall.
Her head is big; her heart is small.
It's hard to find Mr. Right
When she herself is so damn uptight!

So many dates, but nothing is clicking.
Her roots are gray and her clock is ticking.
She has to look young. That is a must!
In front of a mirror she constantly fussed.
Her look isn't natural, like a hippy or a Quaker;
She wears her make-up like Tammy-Fay Baker.
In her effort to find romance—
Botox injections and breast implants.
With collagen lips and boobs that are fake,
She is so skinny she looks like a rake.
If she weren't obsessed with being so thin,

She could've mastered the violin.
In the time and effort she spends on her hair,
She could've become a department chair.

Artificially tan, artificially blonde,
She likes to frequent tanning solons,
Where she can get a body of bronze
Without ever lying on beaches or lawns.
Feeling indulgent when her day is done,
She tans at night, no need for the sun.
Faster still is the spray-on tan,
Where you don't have to lie on that roasting pan.
She picks the color; the tanning is rapid.
This appeals to a mind so vapid.
They spray the brown dye in a big fan,
Till you look like you've come from the
    beaches of Cannes.
Standing stark naked, the self-centered broad,
In a chamber reminiscent of the Marquis de Sade,
Signals she's ready with a very slight nod,
And receives the brown spray like she's praying to
    God!

What is her name? Cindy or Sue?
Maybe she's Tina…. *Maybe she's you!*

Every weekend it's the same;
He drinks beer and watches the game.
Football is a state of mind
Where it's always Miller Time.
Buffalo wings and ranch dressing
Or chips and salsa are a blessing.
On the couch he would gel
While he watched the NFL.
From the comfort of his den,
He never missed the Pac Ten.

RUDE RAGE

He never missed NASCAR.
(He also has a wet bar.)
Players and stats he'd memorize.
"They're a great ball club, a fine franchise."
Being a fan gave his life reason.
"I can't wait to see what they do next season!"

Though he loved things athletic,
He himself was quite hermetic.
For example, he couldn't recall
The last time he threw a ball.
Ensconced in his lair, watching a match
A true spectator, he didn't play catch.
Watching a game, he was content,
But didn't know much about current events.
He flipped through channels with his remote;
Played Fantasy Football but he didn't vote.
He knew about coaches and draft picks,
But not world events or politics.
Regarding the government, he often complained
Of income tax and capital gains.
He didn't believe in social programs;
He'd rather watch the Bears and the Rams.
Complacent with how we live together,
As resigned to the system as he was to the weather,
He never volunteered for a campaign.
His purpose on earth was to be entertained.

He could make the world a better place,
If only he'd turn off the stock-car race.
He could contribute to society
But preferred his Lazy-Boy and insobriety,
Watching the game, being a grouch,
Whiling away the day on the couch.

One night when his team wasn't playing their best,
He suffered acute cardiac arrest.
They found him dead in his Lazy-Boy chair
With a warm beer and a frozen stare.

Sit right down and I'll tell you a tale
About a white suburban male
Who lives on a street in Orange County
Where peace and quiet are in bounty.
But he lives in fear of a nebulous threat
And of things he hears on his TV set.
Guarding his property is his charge;
Guarding from what? Society at large!
Fences, cameras, a series of locks—
You'd think he was charged with guarding Fort Knox.
He secures his perimeters, knows the terrain,
Has many keys on the end of a chain.
His vigilance may seem out of proportion

JOEL FARSON

To those who don't read *Soldier of Fortune*.
Flags fly at his front gate,
Beacons of a security state.
This Sovereign Citizen never relaxes
As long as the government collects taxes.

He harkens back to the good ol' days,
Before Civil Rights, hippies, and gays.
His belly is white; his neck is reddish;
When it comes to guns he has a fetish.
Carrying a semi-automatic
Is his idea of democratic.
In his basement, a stockpile of ammo.
His daddy wore sheets; he wears "camo."

When he shops for guns and weapons of war,
He's like a kid in a candy store.
A sober and reluctant purchase? *Yeah, right.*
When he sees a gun, it's love at first sight.
Eros and *thanatos* wrapped into one—
A death instinct and lust for a gun.

(Owning guns *is* our sacred right,
But our gun-crazy culture is out of sight.)

With mirrored glasses and a walkie-talkie,
He tinkers with guns while watching hockey

And talks with fellow NRA brothers
Who haven't outgrown playing Cops and Robbers.
A race descended from white Europeans,
Who haven't outgrown playing Cowboys and Indians.
They want all foreign people gone
(Except the ones who mow their lawn).
He thinks the Ku Klux Klan is cool.
(His son bullies gay kids after school.)

"We're a civilization in decline.
I'm here to reclaim this country of mine!
Naïve utopians don't understand
That anarchy is imminent across this land!
They'll rape and pillage in angry mobs,
Like a lawless scenario from Thomas Hobbes—
A spectacle full of fear and loathing,
(He's really 'a sheep in wolf's clothing.')

So, get off his lawn. Don't lean on his fence.
He may start shooting in "self-defense." Better play it safe and take off the hoodie.
"He wouldn't really shoot me for that, would he?"
Exit the neighborhood. Don't walk around.
He may decide to "stand his ground."

JOEL FARSON

By day, he's a righteous vigilante;
By night he likes to wear women's panties.
A hypocrite from the far Right—
Sanctimonious by day, queer at night.
And on his radio, from coast to coast,
Is the loud, obnoxious talk-show host
Who's full of anger, full of zeal,
Says he knows just how you feel.
He sees the world in black and white.
It's us and them. It's time to fight!
Inciting violence on the air
To hysterical people, easy to scare.
He's propagating twisted views.
And his brainwashed listeners say, "Me too!"

But the Cul-de-Sac Crusader doesn't panic,
Convinced the future is messianic.
He harbors contempt for most of mankind,
For those of us who'll be "left behind."
No nuance, no shades of gray,
God's will be done! Let us pray....

The Too-muchness of Everything

He got off the couch with a fart,
Grabbed his keys, and was off to Walmart.
His wife, too, likes shopping for stuff,
But no matter how much, it's never enough.
When we feel empty we go to the store
And collect commodities, but who's keeping score?
Compulsive shoppers, we personify greed,
Buying things we don't really need.
On Sundays we pray and make confessions;
On Mondays we pine for earthly possessions.
Instead of giving what's good for each other,
We're seduced by one gadget after another.
Products that will impress our neighbors,
Made in sweatshops with child labor.
We take advantage of the global economy,
Low-paid workers, and corporate autonomy.
For manufacturing merchandise
Is a quest to find the lowest price.
Never mind that American jobs are lost
To people who'll work for a fraction of the cost.

JOEL FARSON

No factory jobs in North Carolina?
Well, half of what you own is made in China.

And do you wonder where the profits went?
They have gone to "the one percent,"
To those patriotic "job creators,"
Most of whom are tax evaders.
Their corporate addresses offshore,
So they can pocket even more.

But if more profits went into *workers'* hands,
The economy would grow by increased *demand!*
A working class with some spending money
Would stimulate business so much it's not funny.

But mom-and-pop businesses shut their doors
While we shop at the "company store."
We shop at Walmart to buy cheap stuff
Because we simply don't earn enough.
Our consumer consciousness isn't deep.
We're simply going to buy what's cheap.
Our unemployed may live in squalor,
"But no one tells me how to spend my dollar!"
We buy what's cheapest on the shelf
And wouldn't boycott grapes for Cesar Chavez himself.

RUDE RAGE

So, frantically we roam the floors
At the big-box grocery stores,
Pushing carts down the aisle,
Weaving through shoppers without a smile,
Reaching for items hand-over-fist,
Crossing things off our grocery list.
Watch us hurry; watch us worry;
We move so fast our legs are blurry.
And though we may have a college degree,
We can't seem to utter "Excuse me."
(Is it "educated" to act so crude?
In Spanish *maleducado* means "rude.")
Must we always push and shove?
Where's the courtesy? Where's the love?
Call me mellow; call me a hippy;
Why is everyone so damn zippy?

Another example of our greed
Is the way we like to feed.
After shopping we might pay
A visit to Home Town Buffet,
Where it's all you can eat for $9.99.
It says so right there on the sign.
Four kinds of butter, six kinds of bread,
Pasta and salad—Oh, what a spread!
Salami and cheese, mayonnaise and mustard,

JOEL FARSON

Soup, salsa, ice cream and custard.
Go ahead, have it your way!
But prepare yourself for a vulgar display.
The way we pile so much food
On one plate is really rude.
Consider the food that some devour,
All in less than half an hour.
If we're going to eat all that,
It's no wonder that we're fat.
We find ourselves in this condition
Largely due to poor nutrition.
Exercise is too exhausting.
(We like cake with lots of frosting.)
We eat too much and lose self-esteem
On the road to the American Dream.

If we really want to be thinner,
Why do we go to McDonald's for dinner?
It's no wonder we're obese,
Eating food fried in grease.
Consider the profit in a can of Coke—
It's no wonder we're fat and broke.
A burger, fries, and a malt?
Lots of sugar, fat, and salt.
A cheeseburger and a shake?
Don't feel guilty; that's what they make.

Onion rings and a malt?
It's what they give you. It's not your fault!

We need a break! We've had enough!
We need a break from all this stuff!
Too much stuff causes stress,
Crowds the house, makes a mess,
Brings our bodies to Death's door.
Haven't we learned that *less is more?*

Yet, the market itself is the first to hype
The virtues of the simple life.
Ironically, we'd be satisfied
With a life more simplified.
Contentment isn't found in things we acquire;
It's found in the *absence of desire.*
So, avoid waste and be dutiful
To the idea that "*small is beautiful.*"
And soon we'll find that we'll be freed
From the things that we don't need.
Enjoying pleasures simple and real
May just help the way we feel,
And then we'll cry out with a sigh,
"There really is a natural high!"

Corporate Cheaters

Todd was not a working stiff;
He was a big executive
Who moved in elite social spheres
With corporate types and financiers.
A member of the *bourgeoisie*,
He had an Ivy League degree.
But in the years he went to school,
Todd never learned the Golden Rule.
He never read *The Grapes of Wrath*
But he was good at fuzzy math.
Thanks to his creative accounting,
Corporate profits were always mounting.
He dreamed of ways that he could win
While at the club, drinking gin,
And lobbying for legislation

That did away with regulation.
Making money for the elite,
Inflating stocks on Wall Street.
Windfall profits off the chart—
What we call cheating, he calls art.

He wouldn't accept making less
By paying out the IRS.
Certain people's palms were greased,
Making sure profits increased.
Todd would often cook the books
With his fellow common crooks.
Even Todd's own protégé
Smiled and looked the other way.
You and I have only dreamt
Of such wealth, tax exempt.
Wall Street made even more
When Todd moved accounts offshore.
By reducing overhead,
Avoiding taxes and The Fed,
Outsourcing jobs—who would've guessed
That stocks go up when you divest?

Corporate cats got more payoffs
With every round of new layoffs.
Todd owned a yacht and private jet.

JOEL FARSON

He fired workers deep in debt.
Americans were out of work,
But Todd got a bonus. (It made him smirk.)
The American workforce is betrayed
In the glorious name of free trade.
Far away from the U.S.
Many people work for less.
We've sold the soul of our nation
To multinational corporations.

But don't despair. Stop complaining!
Go back to school for retraining.
Leave your factories; leave your mills,
Go back to school to get new skills.
Though the factories are rusting,
And politicians are union busting,
You can improve your social stations;
Just fill-out fifty applications.
There's not much else you can do.
It's what they call *Catch-22*.
You may not find union work
With benefits and other perks,
But the service sector is out there.
Have you thought of cutting hair?
The manufacturing jobs are gone,
But you might like a beauty salon,
Or flipping burgers, serving beer—

These are jobs that stay right here.
Or maybe answering telephones
To help you pay those college loans.

It's getting harder to make a dollar.
The middle class is getting smaller.
Politicians bait-and-switch
To cut taxes for the rich.
They pass all kinds of legislation
Defunding infrastructure and education,
But still the national debt will soar
If we cut taxes while fighting war.

When they retire, Mom and Pop
Would like to open their own shop.
Instead they work as Walmart greeters,
Underpaid by corporate cheaters
Who oppose increasing minimum wage,
Yet themselves enjoy a gilded age
Of corporate gambling and speculation,
And hardly any regulation.
For the average worker on the floor,
The CEO can make *five hundred times* more!
A free-market boon, if ever one did exist!
(And people think we're going *socialist?*
Afraid we will perpetuate
Some kind of massive welfare state?)

Our taxpayer money bails out banks;
700 billion dollars, and they don't even say thanks.
Congress gives welfare to corporate bosses
Who privatize profits and socialize losses.
So much for your tax dollar—
"Private luxury, public squalor."

So, Todd was called to appear in court
For a suspicious financial report.
But for any crimes the courts detect,
Todd's answer was, *"I don't recollect."*
If they found any crimes at all,
He simply said, *"I don't recall."*
His plea of innocence was all façade,
He was, in fact, guilty of fraud.
But since he was so well connected,
In this scandal he was protected,
Thanks to false testimonies
From his fellow corporate cronies.
Though his actions truly shameless,
The corporate structure rendered him blameless.
Nobody is going to jail
Because the company is "too big to fail."
Charges were dropped, the case dismissed.
Without even a slap on the wrist.
Not only didn't they prosecute,
Todd got a golden parachute.

RUDE RAGE

Why are so many of our leaders
Really just a bunch of cheaters?
Fair play is just a myth.
"Now, what else can I get away with?"

Picture California long ago,
Before it was part of Mexico,
When mountain ranges were pristine,
And empty valleys emerald green.
Native tribes, like the Ohlone,
Combed the coast for abalone,
Picked their fruit from the trees
And gathered honey from the bees.

Then came Spanish missionaries
Who built the sacred monasteries,

And taught the tribes to kneel and pray
And to work the fields all day.
"The afterlife is your reward!"
They spread the Word of the Lord.

Then the Spanish were defeated,
And the process was repeated.
Indians were dispossessed
As pioneers were moving west.
Native people did impede
The quest for gold and white man's greed.
Native people fell to slaughter,
To smallpox, and to firewater.
Americans moving west
Took the land that was best.
Painful tales of devastation,
Trails of tears, and reservations.
In territories far flung
"White man speak with fork-tongue!"
They shot bison from the trains
To let them rot on the Plains.
The Dakota and the Cherokee
Succumbed to Manifest Destiny.
Railroads built with Chinese labor
Connected cities with their neighbors.
Towns and cities began to grow,
As did the warnings of Thoreau,

JOEL FARSON

Who found some peace on Walden Pond,
While the march of progress moved right on.

Yet, even until Steinbeck's day,
When he wrote of Monterey,
Cities smelled of ocean breeze,
And Orange County was orange trees.
But now the West has succumbed to both
Population and urban growth.
California's rushed routine
Is not laid-back or serene.
Business knows that growth is good:
"Let's build another neighborhood!"
Unconcerned with Mother Nature,
Lobbies in the legislature
Accommodated urban sprawl:
"Let's build another shopping mall!"
Hordes in search of land and money
Flock to the land of milk and honey,
Paving over prairie grasses,
Making way for teaming masses.

The automobile provided autonomy
And stimulated the economy.
The Model A, the Model T,
The Chevy, and the LTD—
Behold our love affair with the car.

It's our identity; it's who we are.
Railroads were torn-up after being bought,
And the West became a parking lot.
But the frontier myth is still alive;
Consider the names of what we drive:
Chevy Blazer, Ford Frontier, Dodge Caravan,
Pontiac and Cherokee, Tahoe and Tacoma,
Rodeo and Ridgeline, Yukon and Sierra,
Expedition and Explorer, Mustang and
 Montana.
Even though the frontier's gone,
The frontier myth still lives on.
Iron horses in a race,
Fighting for a parking place.
Modern coaches spewing smoke,
I can't believe we don't all choke!
We've traded horses for cars and trucks;
The Wild West now really sucks.
An hour commute, there and back?
"Where the heck is my jet-pack?"
We should be living like *The Jetson's,*
But we might as well be wearing Stetsons.

We drive around breathing fumes;
Smog in the valley looms.
Freeway noise is all around us;
Noise pollution does surround us.

And methane gas from landfills,
Deadly sludge from oil spills,
Pesticides and motor oil
Seeping down into our soil.
Urban run-off and debris
Running down into the sea.
Marine life to disentwine
From plastic loops and fishing line.
No white sand and coconuts;
Our beaches are littered with cigarette butts
And little pieces of Styrofoam cups.

Cars display American flags
On highways strewn with plastic bags.
Behold all the philistines
Trashing land that was pristine.
Pack your trash! Take you waste!
Apologize to land disgraced!

We tell ourselves we're going green,
But our way of life is gasoline!
Every day we drive so far,
Isolated in the car.
An hour to work, by any route,
Is not considered a long commute.
Three hours a day behind the wheel,
Stuck in traffic is no big deal.

RUDE RAGE

Traffic moving at a crawl?
God forbid your car should stall.

Rarely do we take a walk,
Even just around the block.
Instead we're breathing in exhaust,
Running late and getting lost,
Braking for a red light,
Getting more and more uptight.
We drive fast because we're late,
Race to the light, and then we wait.
We start and stop all over town,
Speeding up to slow down.
Ten thousand cars with fuel injection
All going the same direction.
A world of weasels, watch us squirm,
Competing like a bunch of sperm.
If aliens ever came from Mars,
They'd think that life on Earth was cars!

Consider, too, the financial cost
And the productivity lost
Of wasting hours in the mode
Of paying attention to the road!
It takes so much concentration
Just to get to our destination.
Think of the productivity we'd gain

If we all weren't trying to stay in our lane.
If we weren't always on the run,
Think of what we could get done!

All the freedom and mobility
Of a car or sport utility
Is a myth! It's insane!
We'd be freer on a *train*—
Free to read, free to write,
Free to sleep into the night.
Free to talk with other folks,
Share some stories, tell some jokes.
Trains foster relaxation—
A certain social cultivation.
We're more inclined to say *"Hello"*
Or *"Pardon me, I have to go."*

Cars foster alienation
From our fellow population.
In the frenzy of trucks and vans
We feel contempt for our fellow man.
Enclosed within our metal shells
Like crazy people in padded cells,
We succumb to road rage
And scream at others from our cage!

Mobility is a paradox
When you're stuck inside a box.

RUDE RAGE

The streets completely shape our lives,
Shape the way we walk outside.
A child can hardly be a rover
Without fear of being run over.
So don't let your boy explore outdoors
Unless you want him hit by a Ford.
Distracted drivers who like to Twitter
Won't see your daughter. They just might hit her!
Stay on your block. Don't press your luck.
You too could be hit by a truck!
And how many of us cry with regret
When these damn cars have killed our pet?
Multi-taskers won't survive
If they keep texting while they drive.
Stay in your square. Conform to the plan!
For you too could be hit by a van!
Imprisoned in our little squares,
We think it's normal; no one cares.
From the time that we are born,
The streets force us to conform.
This is our reality,
But is this how it has to be?

If I could design the public domain
I'd build elevated bicycle lanes.
If we rode bikes we wouldn't be fat.
(Besides, most cities are pretty flat.)
Driving doesn't make us trim,

So we spend an hour at the gym.
We don't ride bikes in fresh air;
We pedal at the gym and go nowhere.
A bicycle that doesn't go
Should be hooked to a dynamo.
Harnessing the energy of this toil
Could make us independent of Middle-East oil.
Wiring bikes to such machines
Could power all the lights of Queens!

Nevertheless, we must drive;
It helps to make us feel alive.
How dare anyone try to steal
Our romance with the automobile!
Our car culture is firmly in place,
As sure as any NASCAR race.
Going green would be nice,
But we're not ready to sacrifice.
We drive pick-ups with nothing on the rack,
One person in the truck, and nothing in the back. We'll buy gas if we have to borrow.
We drill for oil like there's no tomorrow.
And when deposits of crude are lacking,
We'll get them anyway—by *fracking*.

We crank the heater, it's always better
Than putting on a woolen sweater.

We might be green if we were smarter
And had followed the lead of Jimmy Carter
Who put solar panels on the White House roof.
Then 'The Gipper' removed them. What good did *that* do?
One step forward and two steps back?
Our energy policy is *totally whack!*
We should follow the lead of Julia Butterfly Hill
Who knows how many trees a year we kill.
We think we need to harvest trees
Just to meet our paper needs,
But the paper that you read
Can be made from a weed!
And why use so much electric light
When the sun outside is burning bright?
With more glass and good design
We'd read indoors by sunshine.

We seek out nature and rugged experience,
But most of that is mere appearance.
We market adventure and open space
To people who really just want to stay safe.

How can we be so impatient
And at the same time so complacent?
Rugged trucks drive over boulders,
With heated seats and cup holders.

Creature comforts and climate control
Make us fussy, soft, and droll.
With stereos on and seatbelts buckled,
We reach for lattes and we suckle.
Safe within our padded cell
Like hermit crabs inside a shell,
We sip on lattes, lulled by motion—
A bit like floating on the ocean.
A sensual experience, soft as silk,
A mobile crib with mother's milk.
Protected in our padded room,
In fetal position we return to the womb,
Alone with our thoughts, alone with God,
On the road more traveled, one pea per pod.

ACKNOWLEDGEMENTS

I want to thank Fred Renn for coming up with the title for this book (years before its publication), and my brother Jeremy Farson for designing the book cover and chapter headings.

ABOUT THE AUTHOR

Joel Farson lives with his wife in Carmel, California. He teaches college writing and literature, and in his free time enjoys surfing.

Made in the USA
San Bernardino, CA
07 December 2017